COUNTDOWN TO SPACE

SECRET SPY SATELLITES
America's Eyes in Space

Timothy R. Gaffney

Series Advisor:
John E. McLeaish
Chief, Public Information Office, retired,
NASA Johnson Space Center

Enslow Publishers, Inc.
40 Industrial Road   PO Box 38
Box 398   Aldershot
Berkeley Heights, NJ 07922 Hants GU12 6BP
USA   UK
http://www.enslow.com

Library of Congress Cataloging-in-Publication Data

Gaffney, Timothy R.
     Secret spy satellites : America's eyes in space / Timothy R. Gaffney.
       p. cm. — (Countdown to space)
     Includes bibliographical references (p.) and index.
     Summary: History of the development of spy satellites beginning with the
Corona in the 1950s; includes information about space surveillance over the
Soviet Union and secrecy of the program.
   ISBN 0-7660-1402-9
   1. Space surveillance—Juvenile literature. [1. Space surveillance.]
   I. Title. II. Series.
   UG1520.G34   2000
   327.12—dc21
                                                        99-050465

Printed in the United States of America

10 9 8 7 6 5 4 3 2 1

To Our Readers: All Internet addresses in this book were active and appropriate
when we went to press. Any comments or suggestions can be sent by e-mail to
Comments@enslow.com or to the address on the back cover.

Photo Credits: The Cold War Museum/www.coldwar.org, pp. 4, 6;
Timothy R. Gaffney, pp. 26, 33; National Aeronautics and Space
Administration, pp. 9, 24; National Oceanic and Atmospheric
Administration, p. 37; National Reconnaissance Office, pp. 11, 12, 14, 16,
18, 19, 21; Naval Research Laboratory, pp. 27, 28; Space Imaging, pp. 35, 40;
SPOT Image Corporation, p. 38; TRW, Inc., p. 29.

Cover Illustration: Naval Research Laboratory (foreground); Raghvendra
Sahai and John Trauger (JPL), the WFPC2 science team, NASA, and
AURA/STScI (background).

*Cover Photo: The United States' first electronic intelligence satellite: Galactic and
Radiation Background satellite (GRAB).*

CONTENTS

Before spy satellites were used, Francis Gary Powers flew over and took pictures of the Soviet Union. Unfortunately, Powers's plane was shot down by the Soviets during one of his spy missions.

I

Shot Down!

Francis Gary Powers was the loneliest spy in the world.

It was May 1, 1960. Powers, an American intelligence officer, was cruising thirteen miles above a foreign country in a U-2 spy plane. He was higher than any other airplane could fly. Earth seemed far below.

The U-2 was a small airplane. It had one jet engine and long, narrow wings. It was not very fast, and it was unarmed. Only his high altitude kept Powers safe from attack.

Powers was flying over the Soviet Union. The Soviet Union included what is now Russia and several other countries. This large country kept its borders closed to the outside world.

But the United States government knew the Soviet

Union had set off hydrogen bombs. It was building bombers and missiles—maybe hundreds of them. Was it getting ready to attack?

To find out, the Central Intelligence Agency (CIA), a U.S. spy agency, was sending U-2s over the Soviet Union. Its U-2s carried cameras that photographed the ground below. The film was flown back to secret offices in Washington, D.C. The film was studied for signs of military factories, bomber bases, and missile sites.

The CIA knew that the Soviet Union had missiles for

Francis Gary Powers spied on the Soviet Union with his U-2 spy plane. The plane's cameras photographed the country so that the U.S. government could look for military bases or missile sites.

shooting down enemy planes. But the CIA believed Soviet missiles could not reach the high-flying U-2s.

The CIA was wrong. Four hours into his flight, Powers felt something jolt the airplane. A "tremendous orange flash" flared around him.[1] A Soviet missile had hit his plane.

The plane spun wildly. Powers bailed out and parachuted to Earth. He landed deep inside the Soviet Union. Soldiers quickly caught him. He was put in prison for nearly two years. The United States traded a captured Soviet spy to get Powers back.

The U-2 downing was a terrible blow to the United States. It had been caught spying on another nation. Worse yet, it proved that U.S. spy planes were not safe from Soviet missiles. The spy flights stopped. Now how could the United States guard against a surprise attack?

The answer was a new kind of craft, one that could photograph more land on a single flight than all the U-2 flights put together. It would map every square mile of the Soviet Union.

This was no airplane. It was something completely new: a spy satellite.

2

The First Spy Satellite

Satellites circle Earth from about one hundred miles to thousands of miles up. They coast through space, where there is no atmosphere to slow them down.

Experts say modern spy satellites can see details as small as a few inches across. They can tell one kind of airplane or tank from another. Even the earliest spy satellites could spot bomber bases and large missile sites.

The 1950s were part of a time known as the Cold War. The United States and the Soviet Union were building bombers and missiles that could carry nuclear weapons. Each country feared a surprise attack by the other.

When Dwight D. Eisenhower became president in 1953, he formed the Surprise Attack Panel.[1] Its job was to figure out how to learn what the Soviet Union was doing. Within the first few years, the panel came up with three ways to find out. One was the U-2 that Powers would later fly. Another was a superfast spy plane now known as the SR-71 Blackbird. Highest and fastest of all was the spy satellite.

The spy satellite was a bold idea. The space age had not yet begun. Nobody had ever put any kind of craft in orbit around Earth.

But the space age was about to start. On October 4, 1957, the Soviet Union blasted a beachball-sized satellite into orbit. It was named *Sputnik*, Russian for "traveler." The 185-pound satellite carried no science experiments or spy cameras, but it was the first artificial satellite ever.[2]

The news shocked Americans. The Soviet Union's first made U.S. space efforts look weak. Two months later, the United States' first

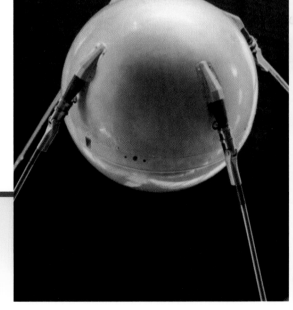

The Soviet Union successfully launched the world's first satellite, Sputnik, in 1957. It orbited Earth and marked the beginning of the space age.

satellite launch flopped. *Vanguard 1* was a gold-plated ball the size of a grapefruit. Its booster rocket lifted it four feet off the pad. Then it exploded. The first successful U.S. satellite was *Explorer 1*. It rocketed into orbit on January 31, 1958.

Vanguard 1 and *Explorer 1* were scientific satellites. Meanwhile, the United States was secretly building spy satellites.

On December 3, 1958, the U.S. government announced the Discoverer program. This program would develop a series of scientific satellites. The Air Force would launch them on Thor rockets. The first few launches would test the hardware. Later ones would carry experiments. Each Discoverer satellite would have a capsule in which to return its experiments to Earth. An airplane would snag the capsule in midair as it drifted down under a parachute.

In the beginning, only a few people knew the truth: Discoverer was really a CIA–Air Force operation. Its code name was Corona.

Corona satellites were made to carry cameras with powerful lenses. Their return capsules would bring the camera film back to Earth. Only a few of the satellites would carry experiments—just enough to support the Discoverer cover-up story.

The Soviet Union was a wide country. To photograph all of it, a spy satellite would need an orbit that took it near the North and South Poles. Because Earth was turning

An Air Force C-119 plane practices catching a target in midair. The United States was ready to start taking spy photographs with the Discoverer satellites. The plane would catch the film as the film canister parachuted through the sky.

inside the ring of the satellite's orbit, each pass of the satellite would take it over a different part of the planet. Several passes would take it over all of the Soviet Union.

The Air Force found a suitable spot from which to launch satellites in northern California. It was a point of land that faced south across the Pacific Ocean. It offered a safe path for rocket launches. The launch site is now named Vandenberg Air Force Base.

Getting into space was still new and tricky. *Discoverer 1* blasted off on February 28, 1959. It was never heard from

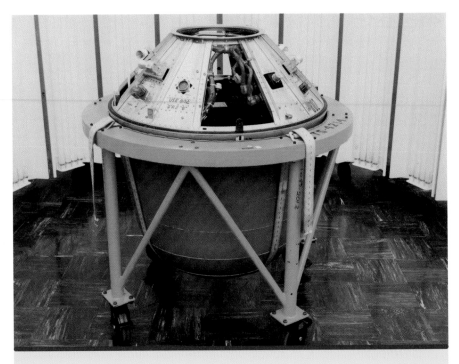

The Corona film capsule, sitting here in its dolly, was a part of America's secret spy satellite. On August 18, 1960, Corona 14 was launched and became the first American satellite to take photographs.

again. Instead of soaring into orbit, "most people believe the *Discoverer 1* landed somewhere near the South Pole," a 1973 CIA report said.[3]

Eleven more flights failed for one reason or another. The thirteenth launch succeeded, but it carried test equipment instead of film. Finally, on August 18, 1960, *Discoverer 14* (secretly, *Corona 14*) sailed into orbit. Its camera worked. Its return capsule dropped the film back toward Earth. But recovering the film would require a tricky midair catch.

3

Catch a Falling Star

Harold E. Mitchell was in the outfield.

The U.S. Air Force captain was flying a C-119 Flying Boxcar over the Pacific Ocean. He was waiting to pluck *Corona 14*'s return capsule out of the sky. So were several other pilots. But Mitchell had been sent to an area five hundred miles south of the "ballpark" where the capsule was supposed to fall.

Up in space, *Corona 14* ejected its capsule. The capsule plunged through the atmosphere. A heat shield protected it. Air friction slowed the capsule down and caused scorching heat to build up. The heat shield briefly glowed like a falling star.

The charred heat shield fell away at 60,000 feet. Out of the capsule popped an orange-and-white parachute. A small radio in the capsule started sending a homing signal.

The capsule had overshot its recovery zone—it was coming right through Mitchell's area. It was about thirty miles from his plane.

Less than two weeks earlier, *Corona 13*'s capsule had also come down right over Mitchell's location. His navigator had experienced trouble getting a fix on the homing beacon. They had missed the catch. The capsule had plopped into the ocean, where it bobbed on the waves. A Navy helicopter and diver had to fish it out. Mitchell did not want to miss again.

Aerial recovery of Corona film return capsule: 1. The capsule has popped out of its parachute. 2. The plane trails a grabbing device from its cargo door. 3. The airplane flies over the parachute. 4. The grabbing device snares the parachute. 5. A recovery crew reels in the capsule.

He flew toward the homing signal. The capsule was 14,000 feet above the ocean when Mitchell spotted it. Time was short. A blanket of clouds hovering at 8,000 feet would soon hide the capsule in white mist.

Mitchell opened the cargo door in the back of the plane. From the gaping hole trailed a pair of poles connected by nylon loops. The loops were supposed to snag the eighty-four-pound capsule by its parachute as the plane flew over it.

Mitchell missed on the first pass. Strike one. He turned the plane for the second pass. He missed again. Strike two.

The capsule was almost in the clouds. Mitchell turned the plane again. Just five hundred feet above the clouds, the trapeze hooked the parachute. Airmen in the cargo bay reeled in the capsule. The film was safe!

Mitchell's crew delivered the capsule to Hawaii. Air Force officers held a brief ceremony near the plane. They honored the crew for recovering the capsule. Mitchell received the Distinguished Flying Cross. His crewmates received Air Medals. Another plane rushed the capsule back to the U.S. mainland.[1]

This was how America retrieved its precious spy satellite film. Once a month—sometimes more often—a Corona satellite would kick its film capsule out of orbit. Airplanes circling over the ocean would wait to snag it out of the air. They seldom missed.

The results thrilled Richard M. Bissell, a CIA official

Colonel Charles "Moose" Mathison shows the Corona 13 *film return capsule to Air Force General Shriever (left) and General White. This capsule was the first capsule successfully recovered, although it was retrieved from the ocean instead of by a plane.*

who codirected the Corona Project. The film from *Corona 14*, he wrote later, "contained pictures covering over a million square miles of the Soviet Union—more coverage than all the pictures of that country taken by the entire U-2 program."[2]

Corona's pictures showed less detail than the U-2's, but they covered parts of the Soviet Union that no U-2 had reached. That first roll of film revealed antiaircraft missile sites, fuel and weapons depots, and new railroad construction.

Less than four months after Powers was shot down, the United States could see inside the Soviet Union again.

The Corona satellites were just starting to show what they could do. From February 1959 through May 1972, the United States launched 145 Corona missions. One hundred twenty missions were completely or partially successful. Counting repeat pictures, the photographs covered an area equal to 557 million square miles—more than eighty times the land area of the Soviet Union.

In 1961, the U.S. government set up a new office to run the Corona program. It was named the National Reconnaissance Office (NRO). Like the satellites, the NRO was kept secret until the 1990s.

In a 1997 speech, NRO director Keith R. Hall told how Eisenhower and his aides prized Corona's photos. "The nation's leaders anxiously waited for the next set of pictures. And they valued the product immensely. If they didn't get their monthly take, somebody got called," he said.[3]

Engineers kept improving the satellites. They made a two-camera system that could make three-dimensional photos. Analysts could then tell how tall objects were. Another film capsule was added so that each satellite could send back more pictures.[4] The photographs

In August 1960, President Eisenhower examines an American flag that was carried in the Corona 13 *capsule. This was the first object that had been returned to Earth from space. The next mission,* Corona 14, *returned the first spy film from outer space.*

themselves got sharper. They could show objects as small as five to seven feet across.

Analysts spotted missile bases, airfields, and storage facilities for nuclear weapons, but Corona's pictures allowed analysts to do more than count weapons. They mapped the locations of the most important Soviet targets for U.S. bombers and missiles.

Eisenhower had started the program to measure the Soviet threat during the Cold War. "The big issue was the

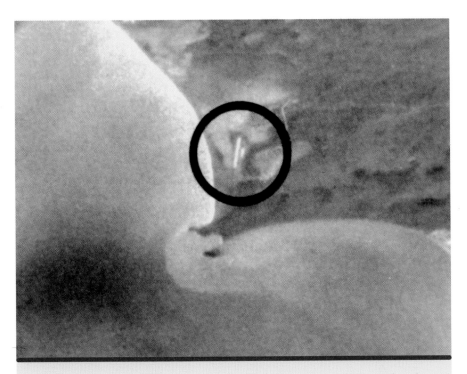

The historic first Corona spy satellite photograph shows Mys Schmidta Air Field in the Soviet Union. The long line within the circle is the runway; the short line is an aircraft parking apron.

missile gap," Dino Brugioni, head of the CIA's spy photo center, recalled years later.[5]

The "missile gap" was a fear by U.S. military leaders that the Soviet Union was building more missiles than the United States was—missiles that could hit the United States with nuclear warheads. The Soviet Union's surprise launch of *Sputnik* fueled that fear.

Corona's pictures proved there was no missile gap. The Soviet Union had few long-range bombers and hardly any long-range missiles. The steady flow of satellite pictures allowed U.S. leaders to keep a sharp eye on Soviet military work.

Analysts watched for signs of new Soviet missiles. Corona satellites often flew over the Soviet Union's Tyuratam missile test center. New launchpads there were a sign that a new missile was in the works. The size of the pads gave some idea of how big the missile was.

Corona's cameras spotted something else at Tyuratam in the 1960s: the Soviet Union's secret program to put a man on the Moon.

Americans and Soviets were racing to put the first man on the Moon. America worked on its Apollo Moon program in the open. It shared its triumphs and failures with the world. That included the program's greatest tragedy: a fire that killed three astronauts while they were training for the first manned Apollo flight.

The Soviet Union worked on its space program in secret. It told only of its successes. But in 1963, Corona satellites spotted the first signs of work on two huge launchpads at Tyuratam. The pads were being built for a rocket even bigger than the U.S. Saturn V Moon rockets.

The Soviet Moon rocket tests started in February 1969. However, four rockets in a row either blew up or failed to reach orbit. Two of them blew up just after liftoff. They blasted the launch site like giant bombs. Corona's cameras recorded the damage. After those four attempts, the Soviet Union canceled its manned Moon program in

The director of the National Reconnaissance Office, Keith R. Hall, says that without spy satellites, the United States would have spent much more money on defense.

1972 without a word. But it had not fooled U.S. leaders.[6]

Military leaders had gained a better idea of what weapons they needed to meet the Soviet threat—and what they did not. "What we spent on satellites, we probably saved several times over in defense spending," NRO director Hall said.[7]

The Soviet Union had its own spy satellite program. The first Soviet satellite to return spy-camera film flew on July 28, 1962.[8]

Both the United States and the Soviet Union kept their spy satellites secret. Yet each knew the value of spy satellites. Each used them to keep an eye on the other.

Spy satellites led to the first treaties between the two nations for limiting their nuclear weapons. Was the other nation building more bombers than their treaties allowed? More missile-firing submarines or missile sites? Each nation could use its satellites to watch the other. Without spy satellites, Hall said, "these treaties would have probably never been signed."[9]

4

Going Digital

As good as the program was, Corona had its limits. It could not take pictures at night or see through clouds. A launch took months to prepare, and each satellite's mission lasted only days—about two weeks at most. Its photographs did not reach analysts until after its mission—sometimes weeks after an event they needed to know about. Corona also could not eavesdrop on radio signals, another effective way to spy.

Events in the 1960s drove home Corona's limitations. One was the Six-Day War in June of 1967. It was a lightning-fast war between Israel and the Arab nations of Egypt, Jordan, and Syria. A Corona satellite went into orbit the day before the war started. Its film came back just eight days later, but by then the war had been fought. Corona satellites could not show U.S. leaders what was happening while the battles raged.[1]

By the 1970s, the CIA was developing a new kind of spy satellite. It would not use film or return capsules. Instead, it would use electronic devices to sense light and make images. These images would be transmitted to Earth as radio signals. The electronic-eyed satellites are widely reported to have been dubbed KH-11 (*KH* refers to the code name Keyhole).

The NRO does not discuss the KH-11, but it confirms the technology is up there. "We can now say there are [electronic] imaging systems, and they began flying in the mid-1970s," NRO historian R. Cargill Hall said.[2]

Observers say KH-11s are a lot like the Hubble Space Telescope—as big as a semi truck and as heavy as ten automobiles. Like Hubble, they have a barrel-shaped body. Inside, huge mirrors gather and focus light into an image. Instead of gazing deep into space like Hubble, however, KH-11s look at Earth.

Hubble can spot galaxies far away. Observers say modern spy satellites can pick out objects the size of a license plate, although they are not able to read them.[3]

Electronic pictures greatly reduced the time it took to get new information. It was an ability President Ronald Reagan secretly praised in 1985, on the twenty-fifth anniversary of the *Corona 14* mission: "I can request photographs of almost any area of the surface of the Earth and have them in my hands in a matter of hours.

By the 1970s, the CIA had a new type of spy in the sky: electronic-eyed satellites codenamed Keyhole. It is reported that the KH-11s are much like the Hubble Space Telescope, shown here.

It is a feat of which President Eisenhower and those before him could only dream."[4]

A KH-11 is said to have taken detailed pictures of a nuclear disaster that the Soviet Union at first tried to keep secret. It was a fiery explosion that ripped open the roof of a reactor at the Chernobyl nuclear power plant in 1986. Deadly radiation spewed into the air and across the countryside.[5]

Another kind of satellite uses radar to make photograph-like images through darkness, clouds, and even the leafy cover of trees. It bounces radio signals off the ground and converts the return signal into digital data. Computers translate the data into pictures.

The NRO does not talk about its radar satellites. However, in 1998 it allowed a CBS News television crew inside a spy satellite assembly plant. The TV crew videotaped a bus-sized spacecraft. The NRO later released its own videotape. News reports said the spacecraft was a radar satellite code-named Lacrosse.

News reports say the Lacrosse program was started in 1986. The goal was to launch a satellite that could spot objects through clouds, darkness, or forest cover. Lacrosse satellites are said to be able to see objects as small as three feet across.[6]

Radar satellites need a lot of power. Lacrosse satellites are believed to have large, winglike solar panels, which turn sunlight into electricity. The Soviet Union made

Space shuttle Endeavour *makes a night liftoff from Kennedy Space Center in Florida. The shuttle was designed to carry civilian and military satellites into space—including the huge KH-11 and Lacrosse satellites, each one the size of a bus.*

radar satellites powered by small nuclear reactors—sometimes with dangerous results.

In 1978, a Soviet radar satellite known as Cosmos 954 went out of control and fell back to Earth like a meteor. Chunks and bits of radioactive metal fell across thousands of square miles of Canada's Northwest Territories. No one was hurt, but the cleanup cost $6 million.[7] Another satellite, Cosmos 1402, fell out of orbit in 1983. People worried that it might fall onto a city, but it came down over the South Atlantic Ocean.[8]

Photographic and radar satellites collect what spies call *image intelligence,* or IMINT. Another kind of intelligence is called *electronic intelligence,* or ELINT. ELINT satellites pick up electronic transmissions from Earth, such as radar signals used to track aircraft and missiles.

The world's first ELINT satellite was launched from Cape Canaveral, Florida, on June 22, 1960. The Naval

A Thor Able rocket launches the world's first electronic intelligence satellite, GRAB, to look for Soviet radar sites that are used to guide missiles.

Research Laboratory called the tiny satellite GRAB, for *Galactic Radiation* and *Background*. The Navy said its mission was to measure solar radiation—natural radiation from the Sun.

True enough. But the satellite also carried a secret instrument to detect Soviet radar sites.

U.S. military commanders wanted to map Soviet radar sites. Radars are the eyes of military air defenses. They are also used to guide antiaircraft missiles. If war broke out, Soviet radar sites would be among the first American targets. Destroying them first would give U.S. bombers a better chance of reaching other targets.

When radar is used to track an airplane, its beam continues into space. From its orbit five hundred miles above Earth, GRAB could pick up radar beams from sites deep inside the Soviet Union. It relayed the signals to a network of small radio huts the Navy had placed

The United States' first electronic intelligence satellite was the Galactic Radiation and Background (GRAB) satellite. It carried secret radar-detecting equipment into the sky.

The Air Force has satellites that are not secret, including this one. It uses infrared sensors to look for missile launchings in other countries.

around the world. Analysts could then figure out where the radar sites were located.[9]

Another kind of ELINT satellite snoops out radio and telephone signals. The government says even less about these eavesdropping satellites. News reports say they listen in on foreign government and military communications. The reports say older ones were code-named Rhyolite, while newer ones are called Vortex. Vortex satellites are believed to have lightweight antennas bigger than football fields for picking up signals.[10]

Not all military satellites that watch Earth are secret. The Air Force has satellites that use sensors to detect infrared light to watch for the hot flashes of missile launchings. Such flashes could signal a surprise attack. Another kind of satellite can detect radiation from nuclear explosions. These have been used since the 1960s to monitor nuclear tests by different nations.

Together, these satellites form a high-flying network of eyes and ears that keep track of military activities around the world.

5

The Secrecy Game

For decades, America's top leaders pretended spy satellites did not exist. But the spy satellite program was never a very well kept secret. Smart observers knew that satellites launched into orbits near the Poles would pass over every part of the planet. The capsules they dropped back to Earth could easily hold film.

Press reports soon guessed that the Discoverer program had a secret side. East Germany, a Soviet-controlled country, called the very first Discoverer launch a military mission. "U.S. politicians and military men are carrying the Cold War into space," an East German news service charged in March 1959.[1]

President Lyndon B. Johnson became one of the most famous spy satellite leaks in 1967. At a party in

Nashville, Tennessee, Johnson talked about the value of spy satellites:

> I wouldn't want to be quoted on this, but we've spent 35–40 billion dollars on the space program. And if nothing else had come out of it except the knowledge we've gained from space photography, it would be worth ten times what the whole program has cost. Because, tonight, we know how many missiles the enemy has.

For the first time, a U.S. president had talked openly about spy satellites. Newspapers quickly picked up his remarks, but the government clammed up again after that.[2]

The secrecy dated from the 1950s. No nation was supposed to fly its airplanes over another nation without permission. It was not clear whether this agreement included satellites. President Eisenhower did not want the Soviet Union to try to prevent the United States from flying spy satellites.

The Soviet Union settled the issue when it sent *Sputnik* whirling over everyone's heads. Soon enough, the United States was sending its own satellites over the Soviet Union. Neither nation admitted that some carried spy cameras.

The secrecy continued for decades.

"That was a big mistake," retired CIA manager Dino Brugioni said in 1998. "That was just foolish. . . . You didn't fool the newspaper reporters."

Brugioni recalled that spy satellites were still secret in 1985, a quarter century after the first successful spy satellite mission. The CIA used the twenty-fifth anniversary of the *Corona 14* mission to honor people who had worked on the Corona program.

"They gave us a medal, those of us who were involved in it. It was called the Pioneer in Space Medal," Brugioni said. "You know what we were told? 'Don't talk about it.' They'd give you a medal and then you couldn't talk about it." He said he showed the medal to his wife, but not to anyone else.[3]

Details leaked out anyway in books, magazines, and

Dino Brugioni, retired CIA manager, stands beside an Agena rocket, similar to the one that carried the Corona 14 *spy satellite into orbit. The spy satellite program was so secret that he was forbidden from showing anyone a medal he received for his work in connection with the program.*

newspapers. And it was all too easy for the Soviet Union to learn even more.

In 1977, Christopher John Boyce and Andrew Daulton Lee were found guilty of selling spy-satellite secrets to the Soviet Union. Boyce worked for TRW Inc., the company that built the Rhyolite satellites. Boyce copied secret papers and Lee sold them to a Soviet agent.

Lee was given life in prison. Boyce got forty years. Their trial drew national attention to the spy satellites.

The Cold War began to melt away in the late 1980s. People in Eastern European countries replaced their Soviet-controlled governments. The Soviet Union itself broke up into several countries. Russia had been the heart of the Soviet empire. Even it replaced its government with one friendlier to the United States.

In the 1990s, the United States began unlocking many of its Cold War secrets. In 1992 it took the wraps off the National Reconnaissance Office. In 1995 the NRO released details about the Corona program. It set up an Internet site with Corona spy satellite photos.

Russia has tried to make its spy satellite program pay for itself. In the early 1990s it set up an office to sell spy satellite pictures through commercial (for-profit) companies.[4]

Today, anyone with access to the Internet can browse what were once the most secret pictures of the Cold War. (Some Internet sites that include these images are listed on pages 45–46.)

This aerial image of Washington Park in Denver, Colorado, shows details as small as three feet across. Tennis courts and bicycle paths are clearly visible. This is the level of detail the latest commercial satellites will offer. The latest spy satellites show details a few inches across.

6

Into the Future

Once a secret spying activity, satellite photography has become a booming business. This is because satellite pictures of Earth have many valuable uses. For example, states and cities use satellite pictures to improve maps or plan roads and utility lines. Mining companies look for untapped mineral deposits. Even video game designers use satellite pictures to make landscapes look more realistic.

As a result, the gap between secret and public satellite photography is shrinking. Several countries have satellites that take pictures anyone can buy. France led the way in 1986 with its *SPOT 1* satellite. In the 1990s, private companies began designing satellites with cameras as sharp as those of early spy satellites. In

Satellites even "spy" on the weather. This is a weather satellite image of Hurricane Mitch made on October 26, 1998. Although the smallest features are more than a mile across, the hurricane's eye is clearly visible in the center of the storm.

September 1999, Space Imaging, Inc. became the first company to launch its own satellite with spy-quality cameras.

Some commercial satellites are good enough for military use. U.S. pilots used SPOT images to practice combat missions during the Persian Gulf War in 1991. The pilots sat at computers and practiced attacking targets in Iraq. These computers used lifelike scenery made from the satellite images. "We were working around the clock to provide that imagery," said Clark Nelson of Spot Image Corporation.[1]

The military is making more use of spy satellites than ever. In the Corona days, the main military use of spy satellite pictures was to find and map bomber bases, missile sites, or other large targets. In the 1990s, military commanders began using spy satellite pictures to target single buildings.

But the United States still uses its secret spy satellites. "The era of the spy satellite is not over," says Jeffrey T. Richelson. Richelson is a researcher for the National

These 3-D views of Northeast Iraq were generated using SPOT satellite technology. With computers, the Air Force can use the images to practice combat missions.

Security Archive in Washington, D.C. "Commercial satellites may never equal spy satellites in resolution."[2] (*Resolution* is the ability to see small objects clearly.)

U.S. spy satellites were busy in the spring of 1999. They spotted targets and photographed bomb damage when the United States and its allies attacked Serbian forces in Kosovo. Kosovo is a region in central Europe next to Serbia. The attack aimed to stop Serbian forces from slaughtering or driving away people in Kosovo who were not Serbian. Thousands of civilians were being killed. Hundreds of thousands fled Kosovo.

During the fighting, U.S. and allied officials displayed pictures taken high over Kosovo. The pictures showed patches of freshly dug soil that looked like row upon row of new graves. The officials believed the pictures were evidence that Serbian troops had killed many civilians. Serbia denied it. After Serbian troops retreated, investigators used the photos to help them look for evidence of killings.

The officials did not say publicly how the pictures were taken, but news reports said U.S. spy satellites took them.[3]

What will tomorrow's spy satellites be like?

No doubt the NRO still keeps some of its plans in deep secrecy. But a test program it is working on with the Defense Department hints at the next generation of sky spies: an all-seeing network of small satellites that make today's large ones seem like lumbering dinosaurs.

The world's first high-resolution commercial satellite photos were taken in October 1999. This one from Space Imaging shows San Francisco.

Under this program, the agencies plan to launch a pair of 3,000-pound satellites around the year 2003. The satellites will cruise in orbits 460 miles high while their radars sweep Earth's surface. They should do much more than just see tanks or airplanes. They should be able to track their movements and relay the data almost instantly to military units around the world.

If they work well, these two satellites could lead to a fleet of twenty-four satellites that would surround Earth. They would keep a nearly constant watch on any point of interest on Earth—day or night, rain or shine. They would track moving vehicles anywhere on the planet and flash the information to military forces. If war broke out, forces could attack an enemy tank or troop convoy almost as soon as it started moving.

The name of this futuristic program is Discoverer II.[4] The name hints at a hope that these spy satellites will be as revolutionary as the ones that were launched at the dawn of the space age.

CHAPTER NOTES

Chapter 1. Shot Down!

1. Francis Gary Powers and Curt Gentry, *Operation Overflight* (New York: Holt, Rinehart and Winston, 1970), p. 82.

Chapter 2. The First Spy Satellite

1. R. Cargill Hall, "The Eisenhower Administration and the Cold War," *Prologue* (Quarterly of the National Archives), Spring 1995, p. 61.

2. Douglas Hart, *The Encyclopedia of Soviet Spacecraft* (New York: Bison Books Corp., 1987), pp. 121–122.

3. Kenneth E. Greer, "Corona," *Studies in Intelligence* (Washington, D.C.: Central Intelligence Agency), Spring 1973, p. 14.

Chapter 3. Catch a Falling Star

1. Curtis Peebles, *The Corona Project* (Annapolis, Md.: Naval Institute Press, 1997), pp. 56, 89–90.

2. Richard M. Bissell, Jr., *Reflections of a Cold Warrior* (New Haven, Conn.: Yale University Press, 1996), p. 138.

3. Keith R. Hall, Speech to National Space Club, September 15, 1997, <http://www.nro.odci.gov/index4.html> (September 10, 1999).

4. Kenneth E. Greer, "Corona," *Studies in Intelligence* (Washington, D.C.: Central Intelligence Agency), Spring 1973, p. 35.

5. Author interview with Dino Brugioni, March 17, 1998.

6. Peebles, pp. 212–215.

7. Keith R. Hall, Remarks to the National Network of Electro-Optical Manufacturing Technologies Conference, Tucson, Arizona, February 9, 1998, <http://www.nro.odci.gov/index4.html> (September 10, 1999).

8. Peter A. Gorin, "Zenit," *Eye in the Sky: The Story of the Corona Satellites* (Washington, D.C.: Smithsonian Institution, 1998), p. 164.

9. Keith R. Hall, Remarks at the Office of Special Projects Alumni Holiday Party, December 6, 1997, <http://www.nro.odci.gov/index4.html> (September 10, 1999).

Chapter 4. Going Digital

1. Curtis Peebles, *The Corona Project* (Annapolis, Md.: Naval Institute Press, 1997), p. 234.

2. Author interview with R. Cargill Hall, October 1, 1998.

3. Timothy R. Gaffney, "Spies in the Sky," *Boys' Life*, May 1995, p. 10.

4. Ronald Reagan, President of the United States, "Memo: Cover letter to William Casey from President Ronald Reagan regarding Corona 25th Year Anniversary," August 18, 1985, NRO Reading Room, Chantilly, Va.

5. William E. Burrows, *Deep Black* (New York: Random House, 1986), pp. 249–250.

6. Craig Covault, "Secret Relay, Lacrosse NRO Spacecraft Revealed," *Aviation Week & Space Technology*, March 23, 1998, pp. 26–28.

7. Kim Rogal and Mary Lord, "A Dying Spy in the Sky," *Newsweek*, January 17, 1983, p. 37.

8. "News Digest," *Aviation Week & Space Technology*, July 9, 1984, p. 26.

9. Naval Research Laboratory, booklet, "GRAB, Galactic Radiation and Background: First Reconnaissance Satellite" (Washington, D.C.: Naval Research Laboratory, no date).

10. Bill Sweetman, "Spies in the Sky," *Popular Science*, April 1977, p. 46.

Chapter 5. The Secrecy Game

1. Guenther Seidel, "Discoverer I Points Up U.S. War Aims," *East German Home Service*, March 2, 1959, NRO Reading Room, Chantilly, Va.

2. Curtis Peebles, *The Corona Project* (Annapolis, Md.: Naval Institute Press, 1997), p. 179.

3. Dino Brugioni, author interview, March 17, 1998.

4. James R. Asker, "High-Resolution Imagery Seen as Threat, Opportunity," *Aviation Week & Space Technology*, May 23, 1994, pp. 51–53; Warren Ferster, "Spin-2 Venture Selling Russian Spy Satellite Imagery," *Space News*, June 8–14, 1998, p. 26.

Chapter 6. Into the Future

1. Author interview with Clark Nelson, March 10, 1999.

2. Author interview with Jeffrey T. Richelson, April 17, 1999.

3. Craig Covault, "Recon, GPS Operations Critical to NATO Strikes," *Aviation Week & Space Technology*, April 26, 1999, pp. 35–37.

4. "Discoverer II," *USAF Fact Sheet*, n.d., <http://www.laafb.af.mil/Special_Interest/disc2/d2.html> (May 2, 1999).

GLOSSARY

antiaircraft missile—A missile designed to shoot down an airplane.

Cold War—A period of tension between the United States and the Soviet Union that began at the end of World War II and ended with the collapse of the Soviet Union in 1991. The Soviet Union is now known as Russia.

ELINT—*El*ectronic *int*elligence. A method of learning secrets by gathering and analyzing electronic signals such as telephone, radio, or radar transmissions.

heat shield—A cover that protects a space vehicle from heating by friction as it travels through Earth's atmosphere at high speeds.

imaging—Making images on film or electronically with visible light or by other means, such as radar.

IMINT—*Im*age *int*elligence. A method of learning secrets by making and analyzing images.

orbit—The path of one object in space around another.

radar—*Ra*dio *d*etecting *a*nd *r*anging. A device that measures an object's distance, direction, and speed by bouncing radio waves off it and measuring changes in the return signal.

reconnaissance—A preliminary survey to gain information, such as a survey of enemy territory.

satellite—A natural or artificial object that orbits a larger one.

space age—The time period of space travel; it began with the Soviet Union's launch of *Sputnik 1* in 1957.

warhead—The explosive part of a bomb or missile.

FURTHER READING

Books

Bachrach, Deborah. *Espionage*. San Diego, CA: Lucent Books, 1992.

Flint, David, Terry Allen, and Nick Skelton. *The Satellite Atlas*. Milwaukee: Gareth Stevens, Inc., 1996.

Parker, Steven. *Satellites*. Orlando, FL: Raintree Steck-Vaughn Publishers, 1997.

Peebles, Curtis L. *The Corona Project: America's First Spy Satellite*. Annapolis: U.S. Naval Institute, 1997.

Internet addresses

Cambridge Research Associates, Inc. <http://www.cambridge.com> (January 28, 2000).
Home page for Cambridge Research Associates Inc., creator of Powerscene. Sample pictures show how Powerscene uses satellite images to make lifelike scenery for flight simulators.

NASA Homepage. <http://www.nasa.gov> (January 28, 2000).
Gateway to NASA's Internet sites. A variety of space images can be found, including Landsat, radar, space shuttle, and Hubble Space Telescope images.

National Reconnaissance Office. <http://www.nro.odci.gov> (January 28, 2000).
Home page for the once super-secret National Reconnaissance Office. NRO's site includes a gallery of Corona spy satellite photographs, cutaway views of Corona satellites, and video clips about the history of the Corona program.

Space Imaging. <http://www.spaceimaging.com> (January 28, 2000).
Space Imaging Inc.'s site shows how satellite images look at different levels of detail. Video clips "fly through" scenery made from satellite images.

Spin-2. <http://www.spin-2.com> (January 28, 2000).
Russia's Spin-2 satellite pictures can be viewed here. They were the sharpest satellite pictures available to the public in the late 1990s.

Spot Image. <http://www.spot.com> (January 28, 2000).
Spot Image Corp.'s home page includes samples of SPOT satellite images.

Microsoft. *Terraserver.* <http://terraserver.microsoft.com> (January 28, 2000).
Home page of the Terra-Server project. View satellite images of different parts of Earth.

INDEX